Introduction

Welcome to "Navigating Niches: A Writer's Guide to Success." In this book, we will explore 20 potential niches that can serve as lucrative avenues for your writing journey. Whether you're a seasoned writer or just starting, these niches offer unique opportunities to connect with readers and create valuable content. Throughout this book, we will provide you with expert tips and insights on what to focus on when writing within each niche, helping you hone your skills and reach your writing goals.

Below is an outline of what you can expect to find in the following chapters in this book.

Chapter 1: Sustainable Living Guides

When writing about sustainable living, focus on practical tips and real-life examples that inspire readers to adopt eco-friendly practices. Highlight the impact of small changes and provide actionable steps for reducing their environmental footprint.

Chapter 2: Digital Marketing for Niche Businesses

In the realm of digital marketing for niche businesses, emphasize the importance of tailored strategies. Teach readers how to research their target audience, create compelling content, and leverage social media to maximize their online presence.

Chapter 3: Personal Finance for Millennials

Writing about personal finance for millennials should simplify complex concepts. Guide them through budgeting, investing, and financial planning while addressing the unique challenges faced by this generation.

Chapter 4: Healthy Aging

Explore the secrets to healthy aging by discussing nutrition, fitness, and mental well-being. Offer practical advice on maintaining a vibrant lifestyle as people age, along with case studies of successful aging stories.

Chapter 5: Home-Based Business Ideas

Provide readers with in-depth insights into various home-based business opportunities. Offer tips on idea generation, business planning, and online marketing strategies.

Chapter 6: Mindfulness and Meditation

When writing about mindfulness and meditation, focus on making these practices accessible to beginners. Describe different techniques and provide guidance for incorporating mindfulness into daily life.

Chapter 7: Vegan Diet and Recipes

Create a comprehensive guide to a vegan lifestyle, including plant-based recipes and nutritional information. Address common concerns, such as protein intake, and showcase the diversity of vegan cuisine.

Chapter 8: Traveling Off the Beaten Path

Inspire wanderlust by sharing hidden gems and unique travel experiences. Include practical travel tips, cultural insights, and offbeat destinations.

Chapter 9: Alternative Healing Therapies

Demystify alternative healing therapies like acupuncture and aromatherapy. Explain their benefits, origins, and how readers can incorporate them into their wellness routines.

Chapter 10: Parenting for Special Needs

Offer guidance, support, and empathy to parents of children with special needs. Share personal stories and expert advice on navigating the challenges and joys of special needs parenting.

Chapter 11: Cultural Cookbooks

Highlight the flavors and traditions of different cultures through cookbooks. Provide authentic recipes, cultural context, and cooking techniques to transport readers' taste buds around the world.

Chapter 12: Crafting and DIY Home Decor

Encourage creativity by offering step-by-step crafting and DIY projects. Emphasize upcycling and sustainable materials to align with eco-friendly trends.

Chapter 13: Self-Publishing Guides

Help aspiring authors navigate the self-publishing process. Cover topics like manuscript editing, book formatting, marketing, and building an author platform.

Chapter 14: Outdoor Adventure and Survival

Equip readers with outdoor adventure and survival skills. Share real-life survival stories, essential gear recommendations, and tips for staying safe in the wilderness.

Chapter 15: Gardening for Small Spaces

Showcase the possibilities of gardening in limited spaces. Offer tips on container gardening, vertical gardening, and selecting the right plants for small areas.

Chapter 16: Learning a Rare Language

Guide language enthusiasts on the journey of learning a rare language. Share language resources, tips for efficient learning, and cultural insights related to these languages.

Chapter 17: Antique Collecting and Appraisal

Educate readers on the world of antique collecting. Discuss identifying valuable antiques, assessing their condition, and navigating the antique market.

Chapter 18: Entrepreneurial Biographies

Explore the lives of successful entrepreneurs. Share their inspiring stories, business insights, and the lessons readers can apply to their own entrepreneurial ventures.

Chapter 19: Mental Health and Wellness for Men

Address the unique mental health challenges men face. Provide strategies for stress management, emotional well-being, and seeking support when needed.

Chapter 20: Unconventional Hobbies

Celebrate niche hobbies like beekeeping and blacksmithing. Offer beginner's guides, safety tips, and insights into the satisfaction these hobbies can bring.

You've embarked on a journey through 20 diverse niches, each with its own unique characteristics and writing opportunities. Remember that successful writing is not only about expertise but also about passion and connection with your audience. As you explore these niches, stay true to your voice, and keep your readers' needs and interests at the forefront of your writing journey. Happy writing!

Chapter 1: Sustainable Living Guides

When writing about sustainable living, focus on practical tips and real-life examples that inspire readers to adopt eco-friendly practices. Highlight the impact of small changes and provide actionable steps for reducing their environmental footprint.

1. Start with a Strong Hook

To capture your readers' attention, begin with a compelling hook or a relatable story. You might share a personal experience of how you transitioned to sustainable living or highlight a shocking environmental fact that underscores the urgency of the topic. This initial engagement will set the tone for the rest of your sustainable living guide.

2. Define Sustainability

Ensure that your readers have a clear understanding of what sustainability means. Break down the concept into its core components: environmental, social, and economic sustainability. Explain how these aspects intersect and why they matter in our daily lives.

3. Make It Relatable

Connect with your readers on a personal level by addressing their everyday challenges and aspirations. Highlight how sustainable living isn't about sacrificing comfort but enhancing it. Share relatable stories of individuals or families who have successfully integrated sustainable practices into their routines.

4. Showcase Benefits

Emphasize the numerous benefits of sustainable living. Beyond the obvious environmental advantages, highlight the financial savings, improved health, and overall well-being that come with eco-friendly choices. Show readers how sustainable living can enhance their quality of life.

5. Emphasize the Power of Small Changes

While the big picture is essential, stress the significance of small, manageable changes. Many people are overwhelmed by the prospect of transitioning to a sustainable lifestyle. Break it down into digestible steps, such as reducing plastic waste, conserving water, or starting a small garden.

6. Provide Actionable Steps

Readers often appreciate practical advice they can implement immediately. Include step-by-step guides for common sustainable living practices like composting, energy-efficient home improvements, or eco-friendly shopping tips. Use clear language and visuals to make these steps even more accessible.

7. Incorporate Real-Life Examples

Real-life examples and case studies can be powerful motivators. Share stories of individuals, families, or communities that have successfully adopted sustainable living practices. Include their challenges, successes, and the positive impact they've had on the environment.

8. Address Common Misconceptions

Sustainable living can be misunderstood. Address common misconceptions, such as the belief that it's expensive or inconvenient. Provide evidence-based explanations and share cost-effective alternatives to debunk these myths.

9. Offer DIY Solutions

Many readers are eager to take hands-on action. Include do-it-yourself (DIY) projects and solutions that readers can tackle themselves. This might include guides on creating homemade cleaning products, upcycling furniture, or building a rainwater harvesting system.

10. Explore Various Niches within Sustainability

Sustainable living is a broad topic that encompasses various niches. Consider dedicating sections of your guide to specific areas like eco-friendly fashion, sustainable travel, or zero-waste living. This allows readers to explore their specific interests within the broader sustainability context.

11. Stay Updated on Trends

Sustainability is a dynamic field with ongoing developments. Stay informed about the latest trends, technologies, and innovations within the sustainability sphere. Share this knowledge with your readers to keep your content current and valuable.

12. Engage with Your Audience

Encourage reader engagement by inviting questions, comments, and suggestions. Create a sense of community around your sustainable living guide where readers can share their experiences and learn from one another.

13. Use Visuals Effectively

Incorporate visuals like images, infographics, and diagrams to enhance the clarity and appeal of your content. Visual aids can simplify complex concepts and make your guide more engaging.

14. Highlight Local Resources

Sustainable living practices often vary by region. Research and include information about local resources, such as farmers' markets, recycling programs, and eco-friendly businesses. Tailor your advice to the specific needs of your readers' geographic area.

15. Promote Sustainability Advocacy

Encourage readers to become advocates for sustainability in their communities. Provide guidance on how to engage with local government, participate in environmental initiatives, and support eco-friendly legislation.

16. Address Challenges and Setbacks

Acknowledge that sustainable living isn't always easy, and readers may face setbacks. Offer strategies for overcoming challenges and maintaining motivation during their sustainability journey.

17. Showcasing Sustainable Brands

Feature sustainable brands and products that align with the principles of your sustainable living guide. This can help readers make informed choices when shopping for eco-friendly alternatives.

18. Foster a Mindful Approach

Encourage mindfulness and intentionality in readers' daily lives. Sustainable living is not just about adopting eco-friendly practices but also about developing a deeper connection with the environment and one's choices.

19. Share Success Stories

Regularly update your guide with success stories from your readers or from the broader sustainable living community. Celebrate milestones, innovations, and inspiring achievements related to sustainability.

20. Stay True to Your Voice

Finally, remember that your unique voice and perspective are essential to your guide's success. Stay authentic and passionate about the topic. Your enthusiasm for sustainable living will be contagious and inspire others to join the movement.

By incorporating these additional tips and tricks into your sustainable living guide, you'll create content that not only informs but also inspires readers to embrace eco-friendly practices and make a positive impact on the environment. Happy writing!

Chapter 2: Digital Marketing for Niche Businesses

In the realm of digital marketing for niche businesses, emphasize the importance of tailored strategies. Teach readers how to research their target audience, create compelling content, and leverage social media to maximize their online presence.

1. Understand the Niche Business Landscape

Before diving into digital marketing for niche businesses, writers should gain a deep understanding of the specific industry or niche they are targeting. Research the niche's history, trends, challenges, and opportunities. Knowing the ins and outs of the niche will enable you to tailor your marketing strategies effectively.

2. Identify Unique Selling Propositions (USPs)

Niche businesses often thrive by offering unique products or services. Encourage your readers to identify their niche business's unique selling propositions (USPs). What makes them stand out from the competition? Understanding and showcasing these USPs will form the foundation of their marketing strategy.

3. Define the Target Audience Clearly

Emphasize the importance of defining a highly specific target audience. Encourage readers to create detailed buyer personas that encompass demographics, interests, pain points, and online behavior. Tailored marketing begins with a deep understanding of the audience.

4. Conduct Comprehensive Market Research

Guide writers on conducting thorough market research within their niche. This includes analyzing competitors, industry trends, keywords, and consumer behavior. Effective digital marketing relies on data-driven decisions.

5. Craft Tailored Content

Highlight the significance of creating content that resonates with the target audience. Encourage the use of niche-specific language and address pain points or challenges unique to that niche. Content should provide value and solutions.

6. Embrace Content Marketing

Content marketing is a cornerstone of digital marketing for niche businesses. Advise writers to develop a content marketing plan that includes blog posts, videos, infographics, and other formats. Consistent, high-quality content helps establish authority and engage the audience.

7. Leverage SEO Strategies

SEO (Search Engine Optimization) is essential for niche businesses to improve their online visibility. Teach writers how to conduct keyword research relevant to their niche and optimize their content for search engines. SEO ensures their content ranks higher in search results.

8. Utilize Email Marketing

Explain the benefits of email marketing in reaching and nurturing niche audiences. Encourage writers to build an email list and create personalized, value-packed email campaigns. Email marketing can help maintain customer relationships and drive sales.

9. Harness the Power of Social Media

Social media platforms are ideal for niche businesses to connect with their audience. Provide tips on selecting the most suitable social media platforms based on the niche and how to create engaging content, interact with followers, and run targeted ads.

10. Invest in Paid Advertising

While organic methods are valuable, paid advertising can accelerate results. Explain the options available, such as pay-per-click (PPC) ads and social media advertising and provide guidance on creating effective ad campaigns.

11. Monitor Analytics and KPIs

Emphasize the importance of tracking digital marketing efforts using analytics tools. Teach writers how to monitor key performance indicators (KPIs) like website traffic, conversion rates, and ROI. Regularly reviewing data helps refine strategies.

12. Emphasize Brand Consistency

Maintaining a consistent brand image is crucial for niche businesses. Stress the importance of cohesive branding across all digital channels, from the website design to social media profiles and content style.

13. Encourage Customer Engagement

Engaged customers are more likely to become loyal customers. Share strategies for fostering engagement, such as hosting webinars, responding to comments, conducting surveys, and running contests or giveaways.

14. Foster Relationships with Influencers

In some niches, influencers can significantly impact brand awareness and credibility. Teach writers how to identify and collaborate with relevant influencers in their niche.

15. Focus on User Experience (UX)

A seamless user experience on the website and other digital platforms is essential. Provide tips on optimizing website speed, navigation, and mobile responsiveness. A positive UX can increase conversions.

16. Embrace Video Marketing

Video content continues to grow in popularity. Encourage writers to incorporate video marketing into their strategy, whether it's through tutorials, product demos, or behind-the-scenes glimpses of their niche business.

17. Monitor Competitors Actively

Staying informed about competitors' strategies and developments is crucial. Encourage writers to regularly assess their competitors' digital presence and adapt their strategies accordingly.

18. Build Trust and Credibility

In the realm of niche businesses, trust and credibility are paramount. Emphasize the importance of showcasing customer reviews, certifications, awards, and any other credentials that establish trustworthiness.

19. Adapt and Evolve

The digital marketing landscape is ever evolving. Encourage writers to remain adaptable and open to new strategies and technologies. Staying ahead of trends can give niche businesses a competitive edge.

20. Measure Success and Iterate

Finally, stress the significance of measuring the success of digital marketing efforts. Teach writers to assess what's working and what isn't, and then iterate their strategies accordingly. Consistent improvement is key to long-term success.

By incorporating these additional tips and tricks, writers can create comprehensive guides that empower niche businesses to navigate the digital marketing landscape effectively. In a world where online presence is increasingly vital, these insights can make a significant difference in the success of niche businesses.

Chapter 3: Personal Finance for Millennials

Writing about personal finance for millennials should simplify complex concepts. Guide them through budgeting, investing, and financial planning while addressing the unique challenges faced by this generation.

1. Start with the Basics

Begin your personal finance guide by covering the fundamental principles of money management. Explain concepts like income, expenses, savings, and debt in simple terms. Ensure that readers have a solid foundation before delving into more complex topics.

2. Emphasize the Power of Budgeting

Budgeting is the cornerstone of personal finance. Show millennials how to create a budget that aligns with their lifestyle and financial goals. Provide practical tools and templates they can use to get started.

3. Address Student Loan Debt

Millennials often grapple with student loan debt. Dedicate a section to understanding and managing student loans, including options for repayment plans, refinancing, and loan forgiveness programs.

4. Explore Income Streams

Encourage millennials to diversify their income streams. Discuss side hustles, freelance work, and gig economy opportunities. Explain how to leverage skills and passions to generate additional income.

5. Teach the Art of Saving

Highlight the importance of saving money regularly. Discuss different types of savings accounts, such as emergency funds, retirement accounts (like 401(k)s and IRAs), and high-yield savings accounts.

6. Demystify Investing

Investing can be intimidating for beginners. Simplify the concept by explaining different investment vehicles, such as stocks, bonds, and mutual funds. Share investment strategies suited for millennials, such as dollar-cost averaging and robo-advisors.

7. Promote Financial Goals

Encourage millennials to set clear financial goals. Whether it's buying a home, paying off debt, or building an emergency fund, goal setting provides motivation and direction.

8. Discuss Tax Strategies

Explain the basics of taxes and offer tips on maximizing tax efficiency. Cover topics like tax deductions, credits, and the importance of understanding one's tax bracket.

9. Tackle the Gig Economy

As a generation heavily involved in the gig economy, millennials face unique financial challenges related to income instability and tax considerations. Offer advice on managing finances in this context.

10. Address Housing Options

Housing is a significant financial decision. Discuss the pros and cons of renting versus buying a home. Explain how to calculate affordability and consider the long-term impact on finances.

11. Navigate Health Insurance

Healthcare costs can be a major financial burden. Explain the different health insurance options available, including employer-sponsored plans, marketplace insurance, and Medicaid.

12. Encourage Retirement Planning

Start early when it comes to retirement planning. Encourage millennials to take advantage of employer-sponsored retirement plans, like 401(k)s, and discuss the power of compound interest over time.

13. Foster a Savings Mindset

Promote a savings mindset by discussing strategies for curbing impulse spending, setting up automatic transfers to savings accounts, and the "pay yourself first" principle.

14. Discuss Emergency Preparedness

Highlight the importance of emergency preparedness. Encourage millennials to build an emergency fund that can cover three to six months' worth of expenses in case of unexpected events.

15. Embrace Technology

Millennials are tech-savvy. Introduce them to personal finance apps and tools that can help them track expenses, create budgets, and invest wisely.

16. Debunk Myths

Address common personal finance myths and misconceptions that millennials may encounter. For example, clarify the difference between good and bad debt and explain that wealth accumulation takes time.

17. Promote Financial Literacy Resources

Point millennials toward reputable financial literacy resources, including books, podcasts, blogs, and online courses. Encourage continuous learning and self-improvement in the realm of personal finance.

18. Discuss Entrepreneurship

Millennials are often entrepreneurial-minded. Offer guidance on starting and running a small business, including budgeting, marketing, and financial planning for entrepreneurs.

19. Address Mental Health and Money

Acknowledge the impact of financial stress on mental health. Discuss strategies for managing financial anxiety and seeking support when needed.

20. Share Success Stories

Include real-life success stories of millennials who have achieved financial milestones. These stories can inspire and provide relatable examples of financial success.

By incorporating these additional tips and tricks, writers can create comprehensive personal finance guides tailored to the needs and challenges faced by millennials. Empowering this generation with practical financial knowledge can pave the way for financial stability and a brighter financial future.

Chapter 4: Healthy Aging

Explore the secrets to healthy aging by discussing nutrition, fitness, and mental well-being. Offer practical advice on maintaining a vibrant lifestyle as people age, along with case studies of successful aging stories.

1. Understanding the Aging Process

Start your guide by providing a clear understanding of the aging process. Explain the biological, psychological, and social changes that occur as people age. This foundation will help readers appreciate the importance of healthy aging practices.

2. Celebrate Aging

Encourage a positive perspective on aging. Highlight the benefits and wisdom that come with age. Dispel common myths about aging, such as the belief that decline is inevitable, and emphasize the potential for growth and fulfillment.

3. Emphasize the Role of Nutrition

Nutrition is a cornerstone of healthy aging. Delve deeper into the importance of a balanced diet rich in fruits, vegetables, lean proteins, and whole grains. Provide guidance on portion control and the significance of staying hydrated.

4. Nutritional Needs for Aging Bodies

Explain how nutritional needs change with age. Discuss the importance of nutrients like calcium and vitamin D for bone health, omega-3 fatty acids for heart health, and antioxidants for cellular protection.

5. Mindful Eating

Promote mindful eating practices. Encourage readers to savor their meals, pay attention to hunger and fullness cues, and be conscious of emotional eating. Mindful eating fosters a healthier relationship with food.

6. Offer Guidance on Physical Activity

Physical activity is key to healthy aging. Provide specific recommendations for exercise routines that cater to older adults. Include options like aerobic exercises, strength training, flexibility exercises, and balance training.

7. Address Common Health Concerns

Discuss common health concerns associated with aging, such as arthritis, diabetes, heart disease, and osteoporosis. Offer prevention strategies, management tips, and guidance on when to seek medical advice.

8. Mental Well-being and Cognitive Health

Mental well-being is vital for healthy aging. Explore the significance of staying mentally active through activities like puzzles, reading, and learning new skills. Discuss the importance of social connections and emotional resilience.

9. Promote Regular Health Check-Ups

Highlight the importance of regular health check-ups and screenings as people age. Encourage readers to be proactive about their health and to discuss any concerns with healthcare professionals.

10. The Role of Sleep

Discuss the importance of quality sleep for healthy aging. Offer tips on improving sleep hygiene and addressing common sleep disturbances that can occur with age.

11. Encourage Lifelong Learning

Promote lifelong learning to keep the mind engaged and active. Suggest activities like taking online courses, joining book clubs, or pursuing new hobbies.

12. Case Studies of Successful Aging

Include inspiring case studies of individuals who have aged gracefully and maintained a high quality of life. These stories can serve as examples and sources of motivation for readers.

13. Address Loneliness and Isolation

Acknowledge the issue of loneliness and social isolation, which can be prevalent among older adults. Discuss strategies for building and maintaining social connections, such as joining clubs, volunteering, or reconnecting with family and friends.

14. Healthy Aging for Caregivers

Recognize the role of caregivers in the lives of older adults. Offer guidance and support for caregivers, including tips on self-care, managing caregiver stress, and accessing resources.

15. Alternative and Complementary Therapies

Explore alternative and complementary therapies that can benefit older adults. Discuss practices like acupuncture, meditation, and tai chi, which promote physical and mental well-being.

16. Stress Management

Stress can have a significant impact on the aging process. Provide stress management techniques, such as deep breathing exercises, progressive muscle relaxation, and mindfulness meditation.

17. Encourage Independence

Empower older adults to maintain their independence for as long as possible. Offer tips on adapting the home environment for safety and accessibility.

18. Promote Healthy Relationships

Discuss the importance of maintaining healthy relationships with family and friends. Explore strategies for resolving conflicts and nurturing supportive connections.

19. Address End-of-Life Planning

While a sensitive topic, it's important to address end-of-life planning. Encourage readers to consider their wishes for medical care, create advance directives, and discuss these matters with loved ones.

20. Encourage a Holistic Approach

Emphasize that healthy aging encompasses physical, mental, emotional, and social well-being. Encourage readers to adopt a holistic approach to aging that nurtures all aspects of their lives.

By incorporating these additional tips and tricks, writers can create comprehensive guides that empower readers to embrace the secrets of healthy aging. Guiding readers through the journey of aging with grace, resilience, and fulfillment is a valuable and compassionate endeavor.

Chapter 5: Home-Based Business Ideas

Provide readers with in-depth insights into various home-based business opportunities. Offer tips on idea generation, business planning, and online marketing strategies.

1. Introduction to Home-Based Businesses

Begin your guide with an introduction to home-based businesses. Explain why they are a viable option, highlighting the benefits of flexibility, reduced overhead costs, and the potential for work-life balance.

2. Idea Generation Strategies

Dive deeper into idea generation. Provide readers with techniques for brainstorming and identifying home-based business opportunities that align with their skills, interests, and market demand. Encourage them to think creatively.

3. Niche Selection

Discuss the importance of niche selection in home-based businesses. Encourage readers to focus on niches where they have expertise or a passion, as this can lead to a more enjoyable and sustainable business.

4. Market Research

Emphasize the significance of market research in validating business ideas. Guide readers on how to analyze market trends, identify target audiences, and assess competition. Effective market research is a foundation for success.

5. Business Planning

Offer a step-by-step guide to business planning for home-based entrepreneurs. Explain how to create a business plan that outlines goals, strategies, financial projections, and a clear path to profitability.

6. Legal and Regulatory Considerations

Address legal and regulatory considerations specific to home-based businesses. Discuss business licenses, permits, zoning regulations, and tax obligations. Encourage readers to seek legal advice if needed.

7. Home Office Setup

Provide practical tips for setting up a productive home office. Cover topics like ergonomics, organization, and creating a conducive workspace. A well-organized home office enhances efficiency.

8. Time Management

Time management is crucial for home-based entrepreneurs. Offer strategies for creating a daily schedule, setting boundaries, and staying disciplined. Productivity tools and techniques can be invaluable.

9. Online Presence

Explore the importance of establishing an online presence for home-based businesses. Explain the value of a professional website, social media profiles, and online marketing strategies for reaching a broader audience.

10. Branding and Identity

Discuss the significance of branding and creating a unique identity. Teach readers how to develop a compelling brand message, design a memorable logo, and create a consistent brand image across all platforms.

11. Financial Management

Financial management is key to the success of any business. Provide guidance on budgeting, accounting, and financial tracking. Encourage readers to separate personal and business finances.

12. Networking and Collaboration

Highlight the benefits of networking in the home-based business world. Share tips on how to build valuable connections, both online and offline, and how collaboration with other entrepreneurs can be mutually beneficial.

13. Marketing Strategies

Explore various marketing strategies suitable for home-based businesses. Cover content marketing, social media marketing, email marketing, and paid advertising. Encourage readers to create a marketing plan tailored to their target audience.

14. Customer Relationship Management

Discuss the importance of nurturing customer relationships. Explain how excellent customer service, feedback collection, and personalized communication can lead to customer loyalty and referrals.

15. Scaling and Growth

Address strategies for scaling a home-based business. Provide insights into expanding the product or service offerings, hiring remote employees or freelancers, and exploring new markets.

16. Online Selling Platforms

For businesses that involve selling products, guide readers on choosing the right online selling platforms. Discuss popular options like Amazon, eBay, Etsy, and the importance of optimizing product listings.

17. E-commerce and Payment Processing

Explain e-commerce options and payment processing systems. Offer insights into secure online transactions, payment gateways, and setting up secure online shopping experiences for customers.

18. Customer Data Protection

Discuss the importance of customer data protection and privacy compliance, particularly when handling sensitive information. Highlight the significance of data security measures and legal responsibilities.

19. Adapting to Challenges

Acknowledge that home-based businesses may face unique challenges, such as isolation and distractions. Share strategies for overcoming these challenges, staying motivated, and seeking support when needed.

20. Real-Life Success Stories

Inspire readers by sharing real-life success stories of home-based entrepreneurs who turned their ideas into thriving businesses. These stories can serve as examples of what is achievable with determination and dedication.

By incorporating these additional tips and tricks, writers can create comprehensive guides that empower readers to explore, plan, and launch successful home-based businesses. The world of entrepreneurship from home offers exciting opportunities for individuals to pursue their passions and financial independence.

Chapter 6: Mindfulness and Meditation

When writing about mindfulness and meditation, focus on making these practices accessible to beginners. Describe different techniques and provide guidance for incorporating mindfulness into daily life.

1. Introduction to Mindfulness

Begin your guide with a clear and concise introduction to mindfulness. Explain what mindfulness is and why it matters in today's fast-paced world. Emphasize that mindfulness is a practice that anyone can learn and benefit from.

2. Benefits of Mindfulness

Dive deeper into the numerous benefits of mindfulness, both for mental and physical well-being. Discuss how mindfulness can reduce stress, improve focus, enhance emotional regulation, and promote overall happiness.

3. Mindfulness vs. Meditation

Clarify the distinction between mindfulness and meditation. While meditation is a formal practice, mindfulness is a broader concept that can be integrated into daily life. Explain how they complement each other.

4. Start with Simple Techniques

For beginners, simplicity is key. Describe basic mindfulness techniques that are easy to grasp, such as mindful breathing, body scanning, or focused attention on the present moment. Encourage readers to start with these foundational practices.

5. Guided Meditations

Offer guided meditation scripts that beginners can follow along with. These can serve as valuable tools for cultivating mindfulness, especially for those new to the practice. Provide links or references to online resources or apps that offer guided meditations.

6. Mindful Movement

Introduce mindful movement practices like yoga or tai chi. These are excellent options for individuals who find it challenging to sit still during meditation. Explain how mindful movement can enhance body awareness and relaxation.

7. Incorporating Mindfulness into Daily Life

Guide readers on how to integrate mindfulness into their daily routines. Offer practical tips for being present in everyday activities, such as mindful eating, mindful walking, and mindful listening.

8. Setting Realistic Expectations

Encourage beginners to set realistic expectations for their mindfulness practice. Explain that it's normal to have a wandering mind during meditation and that consistency and patience are key to progress.

9. Mindfulness in Stressful Situations

Discuss how mindfulness can be particularly helpful during stressful situations. Provide techniques for staying calm and centered when facing challenges, such as the "STOP" (Stop, Take a Breath, Observe, Proceed) technique.

10. Mindfulness Apps and Resources

Recommend mindfulness apps and online resources that can support beginners on their journey. Explain the features and benefits of these tools, including guided meditations, timers, and progress tracking.

11. Mindfulness in Relationships

Explore the application of mindfulness in interpersonal relationships. Discuss how mindfulness can improve communication, empathy, and conflict resolution. Provide practical exercises for mindful listening and mindful speaking.

12. Mindfulness and Sleep

Address the role of mindfulness in promoting better sleep. Offer relaxation techniques and bedtime routines that can help readers wind down and prepare for restful sleep.

13. Dealing with Distractions

Acknowledge that distractions are common during meditation. Share strategies for dealing with distractions without frustration, such as gently bringing the focus back to the breath or the present moment.

14. Mindfulness and Emotional Well-being

Examine how mindfulness can improve emotional well-being. Discuss its role in managing negative emotions, reducing anxiety, and cultivating gratitude and positivity.

15. Silence vs. Guided Meditation

Explain the differences between silent meditation and guided meditation. Encourage readers to explore both approaches and find what resonates best with them.

16. Mindfulness in the Workplace

Discuss how mindfulness can enhance productivity and reduce workplace stress. Offer tips for incorporating mindfulness practices into the workday, such as short breathing exercises or mini-mindful breaks.

17. Mindfulness Retreats and Workshops

Introduce the idea of mindfulness retreats and workshops for readers interested in a deeper immersion. Provide information on how to find and choose reputable retreats or local workshops.

18. Practicing Compassion and Self-Kindness

Emphasize the importance of self-compassion in mindfulness. Guide readers on how to cultivate self-kindness and non-judgmental awareness toward themselves, especially during challenging times.

19. Mindfulness in Nature

Highlight the connection between mindfulness and nature. Encourage readers to practice mindfulness in natural settings, such as parks, forests, or by the ocean. Nature can enhance the mindfulness experience.

20. Cultivating a Daily Practice

Finally, stress the significance of consistency in mindfulness practice. Encourage readers to set aside a dedicated time each day for mindfulness, even if it's just a few minutes. A daily practice can lead to profound benefits over time.

By incorporating these additional tips and tricks, writers can create comprehensive guides that demystify mindfulness and meditation for beginners. Making these practices accessible and practical can empower readers to embark on a transformative journey toward greater presence, peace, and well-being in their lives.

Chapter 7: Vegan Diet and Recipes

Create a comprehensive guide to a vegan lifestyle, including plant-based recipes and nutritional information. Address common concerns, such as protein intake, and showcase the diversity of vegan cuisine.

1. The Basics of Veganism

Begin your guide by explaining the fundamental principles of veganism. Define what it means to be vegan and emphasize the ethical, environmental, and health reasons that motivate individuals to choose a vegan lifestyle.

2. Debunking Myths

Address common misconceptions and myths about veganism. Dispel the belief that a vegan diet lacks essential nutrients or that it's prohibitively expensive. Provide evidence-based information to counter these misconceptions.

3. Nutritional Foundations

Dive deeper into the nutritional aspects of a vegan diet. Explain key nutrients that vegans should focus on, such as protein, iron, calcium, vitamin B12, and omega-3 fatty acids. Offer sources of these nutrients from plant-based foods.

4. Protein Sources

Discuss the abundance of plant-based protein sources available to vegans. Include a list of protein-rich foods like legumes (beans, lentils), tofu, tempeh, seitan, nuts, and seeds. Explain how to combine complementary proteins for a well-rounded diet.

5. Plant-Based Calcium

Address concerns about calcium intake for vegans. Provide a list of calcium-rich plant foods, such as leafy greens, fortified plant-based milks, tofu, and almonds. Explain the importance of calcium absorption and how vitamin D plays a role.

6. Iron-Rich Foods

Explain how vegans can meet their iron needs. List iron-rich plant foods like lentils, spinach, quinoa, and fortified cereals. Discuss the significance of vitamin C in enhancing iron absorption.

7. Vitamin B12 Supplementation

Address the importance of vitamin B12 for vegans and the need for supplementation. Explain the various forms of B12 supplements available and how to incorporate them into a vegan diet.

8. Omega-3 Fatty Acids

Discuss plant-based sources of omega-3 fatty acids, such as flaxseeds, chia seeds, hemp seeds, and walnuts. Explain their role in heart health and the importance of balancing omega-3 and omega-6 fats.

9. Meal Planning

Guide readers on how to plan balanced vegan meals. Provide tips on creating a well-rounded plate that includes grains, legumes, vegetables, and healthy fats. Encourage variety to ensure nutritional diversity.

10. Vegan Substitutes

Introduce readers to vegan substitutes for common animal-based products. Discuss options like plant-based milk, vegan cheese, tofu-based products, and meat alternatives. Offer recommendations for choosing high-quality brands.

11. Embrace Whole Foods

Promote the consumption of whole, unprocessed foods in a vegan diet. Explain the benefits of eating fruits, vegetables, whole grains, and minimally processed foods for optimal health.

12. Label Reading

Teach readers how to read food labels to identify animal-derived ingredients. Provide a list of common non-vegan additives to watch out for and how to navigate ingredient lists effectively.

13. Dining Out and Social Situations

Address the challenges of dining out and social situations as a vegan. Offer tips for navigating restaurant menus, communicating dietary preferences, and preparing for gatherings with non-vegan friends and family.

14. Diversity in Vegan Cuisine

Highlight the incredible diversity of vegan cuisine from around the world. Showcase different international dishes and their vegan versions, emphasizing that veganism is not restrictive but an opportunity for culinary exploration.

15. Nutritional Planning for Different Life Stages

Discuss vegan nutrition for different life stages, including pregnancy, breastfeeding, childhood, and the elderly. Explain how to adapt a vegan diet to meet specific nutritional needs.

16. DIY Vegan Staples

Provide recipes and instructions for making vegan staples at home, such as plant-based milk, nut butter, vegan yogurt, and salad dressings. Homemade versions can be cost-effective and healthier.

17. Cooking Techniques

Guide readers on essential cooking techniques for vegan cooking. Discuss methods like sautéing, roasting, steaming, and baking for optimal flavor and texture in plant-based dishes.

18. Vegan Desserts and Treats

Share vegan dessert recipes that demonstrate the indulgent side of vegan cuisine. Offer recipes for vegan cookies, cakes, ice creams, and other sweet treats that can satisfy cravings.

19. Meal Prep and Batch Cooking

Teach readers the art of meal prep and batch cooking for a busy vegan lifestyle. Explain how to plan and prepare meals in advance to save time and ensure balanced nutrition.

20. Sustainable Living and Veganism

Connect veganism with sustainability and environmental consciousness. Discuss how a vegan diet can reduce the environmental footprint and contribute to a more sustainable future.

By incorporating these additional tips and tricks, writers can create a comprehensive guide that not only addresses nutritional concerns but also inspires readers to embrace the diverse and exciting world of vegan cuisine. Veganism is not just a dietary choice; it's a lifestyle that promotes health, compassion.

Chapter 8: Traveling Off the Beaten Path

Inspire wanderlust by sharing hidden gems and unique travel experiences. Include practical travel tips, cultural insights, and offbeat destinations.

1. The Essence of Offbeat Travel

Begin your guide by defining what offbeat travel means. Explain that it involves seeking destinations, experiences, and adventures that are not typically found in tourist brochures. Encourage readers to embrace the thrill of exploration.

2. Mindset for Offbeat Travel

Discuss the mindset required for offbeat travel. Emphasize the importance of curiosity, adaptability, and a willingness to step out of one's comfort zone. Encourage readers to approach offbeat destinations with an open heart and mind.

3. Research and Planning

Guide readers on how to research offbeat destinations effectively. Explain the significance of in-depth research, including local customs, traditions, and any safety considerations. Encourage readers to plan their itineraries but leave room for spontaneity.

4. Authentic Experiences

Highlight the value of seeking authentic experiences in offbeat destinations. Encourage readers to interact with locals, immerse themselves in the culture, and participate in local activities or festivals.

5. Responsible Tourism

Discuss the importance of responsible tourism in offbeat destinations. Emphasize the need to respect local customs, protect the environment, and contribute positively to the communities visited.

6. Packing Essentials

Offer tips on what to pack for offbeat travel. Depending on the destination, readers may need to pack differently. Discuss essentials like appropriate clothing, travel adapters, first-aid kits, and any unique items relevant to specific destinations.

7. Learning Local Phrases

Suggest learning a few basic phrases in the local language of the offbeat destination. Even a simple "hello" or "thank you" in the local language can go a long way in building connections with locals.

8. Navigation and Transportation

Guide readers on navigating offbeat destinations. Discuss transportation options, including local buses, trains, and unique modes of transport like tuk-tuks or rickshaws. Provide tips on how to use maps and navigation apps effectively.

9. Accommodation Choices

Discuss various accommodation options for offbeat travel. Mention choices beyond traditional hotels, such as guesthouses, homestays, eco-lodges, and camping. Explain the benefits of staying in locally owned accommodations.

10. Culinary Adventures

Highlight the culinary aspects of offbeat travel. Encourage readers to explore local cuisine and street food. Recommend trying dishes that are unique to the region and provide tips on food safety.

11. Hidden Gems

Share a curated list of hidden gems and offbeat destinations from around the world. Include personal anecdotes or stories of travelers who have ventured off the beaten path and discovered extraordinary places.

12. Unique Festivals and Celebrations

Discuss unique festivals and celebrations that take place in offbeat destinations. Encourage readers to plan their trips around these events for a deeper cultural immersion.

13. Solo Travel and Safety

Address the topic of solo offbeat travel. Offer safety tips, including how to stay connected, trust instincts, and maintain situational awareness. Emphasize that solo travel can be incredibly rewarding and empowering.

14. Photography and Documentation

Guide readers on capturing the essence of offbeat destinations through photography. Provide tips on photography equipment, composition, and how to respectfully photograph people and places.

15. Leave No Trace

Discuss the principles of Leave No Trace in offbeat travel. Encourage readers to be mindful of their impact on the environment and to leave natural and cultural sites as they found them.

16. Challenges and Rewards

Acknowledge that offbeat travel may come with challenges, such as language barriers or limited infrastructure. Emphasize that these challenges often lead to the most rewarding and memorable experiences.

17. Sustainable Travel Practices

Discuss sustainable travel practices in offbeat destinations. Encourage readers to support local businesses, minimize waste, and choose eco-friendly transportation options whenever possible.

18. Travel Insurance

Highlight the importance of travel insurance for offbeat travel. Explain the types of coverage readers should consider, including medical coverage and trip cancellation insurance.

19. Personal Growth and Transformation

Share stories of personal growth and transformation that can occur through offbeat travel. Explain how stepping out of one's comfort zone and experiencing new cultures can lead to a deeper understanding of the world and oneself.

20. Encouragement to Explore

End your guide with a heartfelt encouragement for readers to explore offbeat destinations and embark on their own unique travel adventures. Remind them that the world is full of hidden treasures waiting to be discovered.

By incorporating these additional tips and tricks, writers can create a comprehensive guide that not only inspires wanderlust but also equips readers with the knowledge and mindset to embark on transformative offbeat travel experiences. Offbeat travel is about embracing the unknown and creating unforgettable memories along the way.

Chapter 9: Alternative Healing Therapies

Demystify alternative healing therapies like acupuncture and aromatherapy. Explain their benefits, origins, and how readers can incorporate them into their wellness routines.

1. Introduction to Alternative Healing Therapies

Begin your guide with an introduction to the world of alternative healing therapies. Define what alternative healing encompasses and explain that these therapies focus on the body's innate ability to heal itself.

2. The Mind-Body Connection

Discuss the mind-body connection in alternative healing. Explain that many of these therapies recognize the interconnectedness of mental, emotional, and physical health. Emphasize the role of stress reduction and relaxation in the healing process.

3. Historical Roots

Explore the historical origins of alternative healing therapies. Provide a brief overview of their cultural and historical contexts, which can help readers understand the rich traditions behind these practices.

4. Scientific Understanding

Acknowledge that while the mechanisms of some alternative healing therapies are not fully understood, many have gained recognition in the scientific community for their potential benefits. Explain the ongoing research and studies in these fields.

5. Holistic Wellness

Highlight the holistic approach of alternative healing therapies. Discuss how these therapies focus on treating the whole person, not just specific symptoms. Emphasize their role in promoting balance and harmony in the body.

6. Common Alternative Healing Therapies

Introduce readers to a variety of alternative healing therapies, including acupuncture, aromatherapy, reflexology, chiropractic care, herbal medicine, and energy healing. Briefly explain the principles and techniques of each.

7. Acupuncture

Dive deeper into acupuncture. Explain the concept of acupuncture meridians and the use of fine needles to stimulate specific points on the body. Discuss the potential benefits, such as pain relief, stress reduction, and improved energy flow.

8. Aromatherapy

Explore the world of aromatherapy. Discuss the use of essential oils derived from plants to promote physical and emotional well-being. Provide guidance on selecting and using essential oils safely.

9. Reflexology

Explain reflexology as a therapy that focuses on specific pressure points on the feet, hands, and ears to promote relaxation and alleviate pain. Offer tips on self-administered reflexology techniques.

10. Chiropractic Care

Discuss chiropractic care and its focus on spinal health. Explain how chiropractors use manual adjustments to address musculoskeletal issues, improve spinal alignment, and support overall wellness.

11. Herbal Medicine

Introduce readers to herbal medicine and the use of plant-based remedies for various health concerns. Discuss the importance of consulting with an herbalist or healthcare professional for personalized advice.

12. Energy Healing

Discuss energy healing therapies like Reiki and Qigong. Explain how these therapies work with the body's energy systems to promote balance and healing. Offer insights into what to expect during energy healing sessions.

13. Benefits and Effectiveness

Highlight the potential benefits of alternative healing therapies. Discuss their effectiveness in addressing specific conditions, such as pain management, stress reduction, anxiety relief, and improved sleep.

14. Safety and Precautions

Provide safety guidelines for readers interested in trying alternative healing therapies. Emphasize the importance of consulting with qualified practitioners and discussing any underlying health conditions.

15. Incorporating Alternative Healing into Daily Life

Guide readers on how to incorporate elements of alternative healing into their daily routines. Offer practical tips, such as creating a calming environment, practicing relaxation techniques, and exploring self-care rituals.

16. Finding Qualified Practitioners

Offer advice on how to find qualified practitioners for alternative healing therapies. Encourage readers to research and choose practitioners with appropriate certifications and experience.

17. Personal Testimonials

Include personal testimonials from individuals who have benefited from alternative healing therapies. These stories can provide real-world examples of the positive impact of these practices.

18. Exploring Complementary Therapies

Encourage readers to explore complementary therapies alongside conventional medical treatment. Discuss how alternative healing therapies can work in conjunction with traditional medicine to support overall wellness.

19. Mindfulness and Meditation

Discuss the synergy between alternative healing therapies and mindfulness or meditation practices. Explain how these approaches can enhance the therapeutic effects and promote relaxation.

20. Encouragement to Explore

End your guide with encouragement for readers to explore alternative healing therapies as part of their wellness journey. Remind them that these therapies offer holistic approaches to well-being that can complement their existing health practices.

By incorporating these additional tips and tricks, writers can create a comprehensive guide that demystifies alternative healing therapies, offers insights into their benefits, and empowers readers to explore these approaches to holistic well-being. Alternative healing therapies have a rich history and continue to provide valuable options for individuals seeking natural and holistic methods of healing and wellness.

Chapter 10: Parenting for Special Needs

Offer guidance, support, and empathy to parents of children with special needs. Share personal stories and expert advice on navigating the challenges and joys of special needs parenting.

1. Understanding Special Needs

Begin your guide by explaining the concept of special needs. Define what it means and emphasize that it encompasses a wide range of conditions, from developmental disabilities to physical challenges and chronic illnesses.

2. Emphasize Empathy and Compassion

Highlight the importance of empathy and compassion when writing about special needs parenting. Encourage readers to approach this journey with an open heart and the understanding that every child is unique.

3. Personal Stories and Experiences

Incorporate personal stories and experiences from parents who are raising children with special needs. These real-life accounts can provide comfort and relatability to readers facing similar challenges.

4. Navigating Diagnosis

Offer guidance on navigating the diagnosis process. Explain the importance of seeking early intervention and the benefits of a timely diagnosis in accessing necessary support and services.

5. Building a Support Network

Discuss the significance of building a support network. Encourage readers to connect with other parents facing similar challenges, join support groups, and seek guidance from professionals and specialists.

6. Emotional Well-being

Address the emotional well-being of parents. Recognize that special needs parenting can be emotionally demanding. Provide strategies for self-care, stress management, and seeking emotional support.

7. Accessing Resources

Guide parents on how to access resources and services for their child. Explain the importance of understanding the rights and entitlements of children with special needs, including Individualized Education Programs (IEPs) and therapy services.

8. Advocacy for Your Child

Discuss the role of advocacy in special needs parenting. Encourage parents to become strong advocates for their child's needs, both within the education system and in healthcare settings.

9. Inclusive Education

Explain the importance of inclusive education and the benefits of integrating children with special needs into mainstream schools whenever possible. Discuss strategies for effective communication with educators.

10. Communication with Healthcare Providers

Provide guidance on effective communication with healthcare providers. Encourage parents to ask questions, seek second opinions if necessary, and become active participants in their child's healthcare.

11. Celebrating Milestones

Celebrate the milestones and achievements of children with special needs. Share stories of triumph and progress to inspire hope and resilience in parents.

12. Promoting Independence

Discuss strategies for promoting independence in children with special needs. Offer advice on fostering life skills and self-confidence, even in the face of challenges.

13. Sibling Support

Acknowledge the impact of special needs on siblings. Offer guidance on how to support and involve siblings in their brother or sister's care while ensuring they receive attention and understanding.

14. Dealing with Grief and Loss

Recognize that parents of children with special needs may experience grief and loss. Discuss coping mechanisms and the importance of seeking professional help when needed.

15. Financial and Legal Considerations

Address the financial and legal aspects of special needs parenting. Explain the importance of financial planning, setting up trusts, and understanding government assistance programs.

16. Assistive Technology

Discuss the role of assistive technology in supporting children with special needs. Highlight the potential benefits of technological aids and resources available for parents.

17. Inclusion in Community Activities

Encourage parents to involve their child in community activities and events. Discuss the importance of creating opportunities for socialization and inclusion.

18. Transition Planning

Explain the significance of transition planning for children with special needs as they reach adulthood. Offer guidance on preparing for the transition from school to post-school life.

19. Seeking Joy and Connection

Emphasize the importance of seeking joy and connection in the parenting journey. Share stories of moments of joy, connection, and love that parents have experienced.

20. Encouragement and Hope

End your guide with a message of encouragement and hope. Remind parents that they are not alone on this journey and that with love, support, and determination, they can help their child reach their fullest potential.

By incorporating these additional tips and tricks, writers can create a comprehensive guide that offers valuable insights, support, and empathy to parents of children with special needs. Special needs parenting is a journey filled with challenges, but it's also a journey where love, resilience, and the strength of the human spirit shine brightly.

Chapter 11: Cultural Cookbooks

Highlight the flavors and traditions of different cultures through cookbooks. Provide authentic recipes, cultural context, and cooking techniques to transport readers' taste buds around the world.

1. Research and Authenticity

Emphasize the importance of thorough research when writing a cultural cookbook. Encourage writers to delve deep into the culinary traditions, history, and ingredients of the culture they are featuring. Authenticity is key to capturing the essence of a cuisine.

2. Culinary Anthropology

Introduce the concept of culinary anthropology to writers. Explain that food is not just sustenance but a reflection of culture, history, and identity. Encourage writers to explore the cultural significance of dishes and ingredients.

3. Regional Variations

Highlight the regional variations within a culture's cuisine. Many cultures have diverse culinary traditions depending on the geography, climate, and local ingredients. Showcase these regional nuances to provide a comprehensive view of the cuisine.

4. Personal Stories

Encourage writers to share personal stories and experiences related to the culture they are featuring. These anecdotes can add depth and a personal touch to the cookbook, making it more relatable and engaging.

5. Ingredient Glossary

Include an ingredient glossary that explains the unique ingredients used in the featured cuisine. Provide descriptions, translations, and possible substitutions for ingredients that may be less familiar to readers.

6. Cultural Context

Provide cultural context for the recipes. Explain the significance of certain dishes in celebrations, rituals, or daily life. Share stories or legends related to specific recipes to enrich the reader's understanding.

7. Cooking Techniques

Discuss essential cooking techniques specific to the cuisine. Explain methods for marinating, grilling, sautéing, and other culinary practices unique to the culture.

8. Traditional Tools

Introduce traditional cooking tools and utensils used in the cuisine. Explain their purposes and provide alternatives for readers who may not have access to specific equipment.

9. Etiquette and Dining Customs

Include information on dining etiquette and customs associated with the culture. Explain table manners, the order of serving dishes, and any traditions related to communal dining.

10. Seasonal and Festive Recipes

Highlight seasonal and festive recipes that are significant to the culture. Provide information on when and why these dishes are typically enjoyed. Include recipes for special occasions and celebrations.

11. Family and Community Recipes

Encourage writers to seek out family and community recipes that have been passed down through generations. These recipes often carry the essence of a culture's culinary heritage.

12. Dietary Considerations

Discuss any dietary considerations or restrictions commonly observed in the culture. Provide options for vegetarian, vegan, or gluten-free versions of traditional dishes when applicable.

13. Fusion and Modern Interpretations

Acknowledge that cuisines are dynamic and constantly evolving. Encourage writers to explore fusion dishes or modern interpretations that incorporate traditional flavors into contemporary cooking.

14. Stunning Food Photography

Highlight the importance of visually appealing food photography. Good food photography can inspire readers and make the cookbook more engaging. Encourage writers to use natural light and food styling techniques.

15. Recipe Testing

Emphasize the significance of thorough recipe testing. Every recipe should be tested multiple times to ensure accuracy and taste. Encourage writers to document any adjustments or variations that arise during testing.

16. Cultural Stories

Include stories about the culture's culinary history, legendary chefs, or iconic food markets. These narratives can provide readers with a deeper appreciation of the cuisine.

17. Ingredient Sourcing

Provide tips on where to source specific ingredients, especially if they are rare or unique to the culture. Suggest online stores, local markets, or international grocery stores.

18. Wine and Beverage Pairings

For cultures that have traditional beverages like wine, tea, or spirits, offer guidance on pairings with the featured recipes. Explain the harmony between food and drink in the culture.

19. Cooking Tips and Hacks

Include cooking tips and hacks specific to the cuisine. These can help readers navigate unique techniques or ingredients more easily.

20. Cultural Exploration

Encourage readers to not only cook but also explore the culture further. Suggest books, films, music, and travel destinations that can complement their culinary journey and provide a more immersive cultural experience.

By incorporating these additional tips and tricks, writers can create a cultural cookbook that goes beyond recipes and becomes a rich exploration of a culture's culinary heritage. Such cookbooks have the power to transport readers to different corners of the world, fostering an appreciation for diversity and the joys of global cuisine.

Chapter 12: Crafting and DIY Home Decor

Encourage creativity by offering step-by-step crafting and DIY projects. Emphasize upcycling and sustainable materials to align with eco-friendly trends.

1. Creative Inspiration

Begin your chapter by emphasizing the value of creative inspiration. Encourage writers to draw inspiration from various sources, including nature, art, culture, and personal experiences. Inspire them to think outside the box.

2. Eco-Friendly Crafting

Highlight the importance of using eco-friendly and sustainable materials in crafting and DIY projects. Emphasize the role of upcycling, recycling, and repurposing materials to reduce waste and environmental impact.

3. Sustainability Trends

Discuss current sustainability trends in crafting and home decor. Explore topics like minimalism, zero waste, and the use of natural materials. Encourage writers to align their projects with these trends.

4. Step-by-Step Instructions

Provide clear and detailed step-by-step instructions for each crafting and DIY project. Include high-quality images or diagrams to illustrate each step, making it easy for readers to follow along.

5. Beginner-Friendly Projects

Include a variety of beginner-friendly projects to cater to readers of all skill levels. Start with simple projects that require minimal tools and gradually introduce more complex ideas.

6. Material Sourcing

Offer tips on where to source eco-friendly materials for crafting projects. Suggest local thrift stores, online marketplaces, or even repurposing items from around the house. Encourage readers to think creatively about material sources.

7. Safety Precautions

Emphasize safety precautions when working on crafting and DIY projects. Provide guidelines on using tools, handling materials, and ensuring a safe workspace.

8. Budget-Friendly Options

Highlight budget-friendly options for crafting and DIY projects. Offer alternatives for readers who may not want to invest in expensive materials or tools.

9. Personalization

Encourage readers to add their personal touch to each project. Share ideas for customizing designs, colors, and patterns to match their unique style and preferences.

10. Sustainable Crafting Tools

Discuss sustainable options for crafting tools. Mention eco-friendly alternatives to common crafting tools, such as bamboo knitting needles or recycled paper cutting mats.

11. Repurposing Old Furniture

Guide readers on how to repurpose old furniture items into stylish and functional pieces. Explain techniques like sanding, painting, and upholstery to transform worn-out pieces into like-new creations.

12. Natural Home Decor

Explore the use of natural elements in home decor. Offer DIY projects using materials like driftwood, seashells, dried flowers, and reclaimed wood to bring a touch of nature indoors.

13. Energy-Efficient Lighting

Discuss DIY lighting projects that focus on energy efficiency. Provide instructions for creating energy-saving lampshades, LED light fixtures, and solar-powered outdoor lighting.

14. Eco-Friendly Textiles

Introduce eco-friendly textile projects such as handmade organic cotton cushions, natural dyeing techniques, and sustainable fabric wall hangings.

15. Indoor Plant Decor

Highlight the benefits of indoor plants for air quality and aesthetics. Offer DIY plant decor projects like macramé plant hangers, terrariums, and repurposed planters.

16. Seasonal Decor

Include seasonal decor projects that celebrate holidays and special occasions. Provide ideas for sustainable and reusable decorations that can be enjoyed year after year.

17. Outdoor Upcycling

Discuss upcycling projects for outdoor spaces. Encourage readers to repurpose old pallets into garden furniture, create DIY birdhouses, or craft outdoor art installations.

18. Sustainability Challenges

Challenge readers to embrace sustainability as a central theme in their crafting and DIY endeavors. Provide creative challenges that encourage eco-friendly choices in materials, processes, and design.

19. Community and Sharing

Promote community and sharing within the crafting and DIY home decor community. Encourage readers to join crafting circles, participate in local workshops, and share their creations online for inspiration.

20. The Joy of Handmade

End your chapter by celebrating the joy of handmade decor. Remind readers that crafting, and DIY projects not only enhance their homes but also provide a sense of accomplishment and fulfillment.

By incorporating these additional tips and tricks, writers can create a crafting and DIY home decor chapter that inspires creativity, fosters sustainability, and empowers readers to transform their living spaces with eco-friendly and handmade creations. Crafting and DIY home decor is not only about beautifying homes but also about embracing a sustainable and creative lifestyle.

Chapter 13: Self-Publishing Guides

Help aspiring authors navigate the self-publishing process. Cover topics like manuscript editing, book formatting, marketing, and building an author platform.

1. Empowering Aspiring Authors

Begin your chapter by emphasizing the empowerment that self-publishing offers to aspiring authors. Explain that it provides creative control, flexibility, and the opportunity to share their work with a global audience.

2. Clear and Actionable Steps

Provide clear and actionable steps for each stage of the self-publishing process. Break down complex tasks like manuscript editing, formatting, and marketing into manageable actions.

3. Manuscript Editing

Discuss the importance of professional manuscript editing. Offer guidance on finding and hiring qualified editors who can help authors polish their work, correct errors, and ensure readability.

4. Beta Readers and Feedback

Encourage authors to seek feedback from beta readers before finalizing their manuscripts. Explain the benefits of diverse perspectives and constructive criticism in improving the quality of the book.

5. Cover Design and Formatting

Guide authors on cover design and book formatting. Discuss the significance of an eye-catching cover and offer tips on formatting the interior for print and digital versions.

6. Self-Publishing Platforms

Introduce various self-publishing platforms, such as Amazon Kindle Direct Publishing (KDP), IngramSpark, and Smashwords. Explain the pros and cons of each platform and guide authors in selecting the most suitable one for their needs.

7. ISBN and Copyright

Explain the importance of obtaining ISBNs (International Standard Book Numbers) for books. Offer guidance on copyright registration to protect authors' intellectual property.

8. Pricing Strategies

Discuss pricing strategies for eBooks and print-on-demand (POD) books. Encourage authors to research market trends and competitors to determine an appropriate price point.

9. Author Branding and Platform Building

Highlight the significance of author branding and platform building. Explain that establishing an online presence through a website, social media, and author profiles can help authors connect with readers and market their work effectively.

10. Marketing and Promotion

Delve into marketing and promotional strategies for self-published books. Discuss book launches, pre-orders, email marketing, social media campaigns, and book reviews as tools for building awareness and sales.

11. Building a Reader Community

Emphasize the importance of building a loyal reader community. Encourage authors to engage with readers through newsletters, author events, and reader giveaways to foster connections and word-of-mouth marketing.

12. Distribution Channels

Discuss distribution options for self-published books beyond online platforms. Explore opportunities for getting books into local bookstores, libraries, and other offline channels.

13. Print-on-Demand and eBooks

Explain the benefits of print-on-demand (POD) for physical copies and eBooks for digital distribution. Discuss the advantages of reaching a global audience through eBook platforms.

14. Book Launch Strategies

Offer tips on planning and executing a successful book launch. Discuss timing, promotion, and the importance of creating buzz around the release.

15. Budgeting and Financial Considerations

Discuss budgeting for self-publishing, covering expenses such as editing, cover design, marketing, and distribution. Encourage authors to create a financial plan to ensure they don't overspend.

16. Handling Rejections and Criticism

Prepare authors for the possibility of rejection or negative feedback. Encourage resilience and the ability to learn from criticism and setbacks.

17. Success Stories

Share success stories of self-published authors who have achieved recognition and success in their genres. These real-life examples can inspire and motivate aspiring authors.

18. Legal Considerations

Provide information on legal considerations for self-published authors, such as contracts with freelancers, taxes, and rights management.

19. Continuing Education

Encourage authors to continue learning about the publishing industry and marketing trends. Suggest resources, courses, and books that can help them stay informed and adapt to changes.

20. Persistence and Patience

End your chapter by emphasizing the importance of persistence and patience in the self-publishing journey. Remind authors that success may not come overnight, but with dedication and continuous improvement, they can achieve their publishing goals.

By incorporating these additional tips and tricks, writers can create a comprehensive self-publishing guide that equips aspiring authors with the knowledge and confidence to embark on their self-publishing journey. Self-publishing is a path to creative independence and the potential for literary success, and it's essential to provide authors with the tools and guidance they need to navigate it successfully.

Chapter 14: Outdoor Adventure and Survival

Equip readers with outdoor adventure and survival skills. Share real-life survival stories, essential gear recommendations, and tips for staying safe in the wilderness.

1. The Spirit of Adventure

Begin your chapter by conveying the spirit of adventure. Inspire readers to explore the natural world, embrace challenges, and develop a deep appreciation for the wilderness.

2. Safety First

Emphasize the paramount importance of safety in outdoor adventures. Encourage readers to prioritize safety by being prepared, informed, and vigilant during their outdoor pursuits.

3. Wilderness Ethics

Discuss wilderness ethics and responsible outdoor practices. Promote Leave No Trace principles, respect for wildlife, and responsible campfire and waste disposal.

4. Real-Life Survival Stories

Share compelling real-life survival stories to illustrate the importance of preparation and quick thinking in challenging situations. These stories can captivate readers and serve as powerful examples.

5. The Rule of Threes

Explain the Rule of Threes in survival situations. Highlight that a person can typically survive:

- 3 minutes without air

- 3 hours without shelter in extreme conditions

- 3 days without water

- 3 weeks without food

6. Outdoor Gear Essentials

Provide a comprehensive list of outdoor gear essentials, including clothing, shelter, navigation tools, first aid supplies, fire-starting equipment, and communication devices. Explain the significance of each item.

7. Shelter Building

Offer instructions on how to build different types of shelters in the wilderness, from simple lean-tos to more elaborate structures. Include tips for selecting appropriate sites and materials.

8. Fire-Making Techniques

Discuss various fire-making techniques, such as using flint and steel, fire starters, and friction methods like the bow drill or fire plough. Emphasize fire's significance for warmth, cooking, and signaling for help.

9. Water Sourcing and Purification

Guide readers on how to find and purify water in the wilderness. Discuss techniques like boiling, chemical treatment, and portable filters. Emphasize the dangers of drinking untreated water.

10. Navigation Skills

Teach basic navigation skills using tools like maps, compasses, and GPS devices. Explain how to read topographic maps, identify landmarks, and plan routes.

11. Food Procurement

Discuss food procurement in the wild, including hunting, fishing, trapping, and foraging. Highlight the importance of knowledge in identifying edible plants and wildlife.

12. First Aid and Medical Training

Encourage readers to gain basic first aid and wilderness medical training. Provide information on treating common injuries and illnesses in remote environments.

13. Signaling for Help

Discuss signaling techniques for attracting attention in emergency situations. Explain the use of whistles, mirrors, signal fires, and electronic devices like satellite communicators.

14. Wildlife Awareness

Educate readers on wildlife awareness and safety. Discuss how to avoid confrontations with wildlife, respond to encounters, and protect food from bears and other animals.

15. Trip Planning and Leave No Trace

Guide readers on how to plan outdoor trips effectively. Emphasize the importance of informed decision-making, sharing itineraries with trusted individuals, and leaving a trail of breadcrumbs.

16. Survival Psychology

Explore the psychology of survival. Explain the importance of maintaining a positive mindset, managing fear and stress, and setting goals in survival situations.

17. Survival Kits

Offer guidance on assembling personalized survival kits tailored to the reader's specific needs and the environment they will be exploring.

18. Staying Calm Under Pressure

Discuss techniques for staying calm and composed during high-stress situations. Encourage readers to practice mindfulness and deep breathing exercises.

19. Evacuation and Rescue Protocols

Provide information on evacuation and rescue protocols. Explain how to signal for rescue, communicate with search and rescue teams, and prepare for evacuation.

20. Learning from Nature

End your chapter by encouraging readers to learn from nature and embrace its lessons. Discuss the profound wisdom that the wilderness imparts about self-sufficiency, adaptability, and the interconnectedness of life.

By incorporating these additional tips and tricks, writers can create a comprehensive guide to outdoor adventure and survival that not only equips readers with vital skills but also instills a deep respect for nature and the importance of responsible outdoor exploration. The wilderness offers boundless opportunities for adventure, self-discovery, and growth, and with the right knowledge, readers can embark on outdoor journeys with confidence and safety in mind.

Chapter 15: Gardening for Small Spaces

Showcase the possibilities of gardening in limited spaces. Offer tips on container gardening, vertical gardening, and selecting the right plants for small areas.

1. Embrace Small-Scale Gardening

Begin your chapter by encouraging readers to embrace the beauty of small-scale gardening. Highlight that limited space doesn't mean limited possibilities and that gardening can thrive in even the tiniest of spaces.

2. Container Gardening Mastery

Dive into the world of container gardening. Offer expert tips on selecting the right containers, choosing the appropriate soil mix, and ensuring proper drainage. Discuss the advantages of container gardening, such as mobility and flexibility.

3. Vertical Gardening Solutions

Introduce readers to vertical gardening techniques. Explore creative ways to utilize walls, fences, trellises, and hanging structures to maximize growing space. Share ideas for vertical gardens that can beautify both indoor and outdoor areas.

4. Plant Selection and Placement

Guide readers on choosing the right plants for small spaces. Emphasize the importance of selecting compact or dwarf varieties that thrive in confined environments. Provide recommendations for both ornamental and edible plants.

5. The Art of Potted Plants

Discuss the art of arranging potted plants. Offer guidance on creating visually appealing and harmonious arrangements that make the most of available space. Share ideas for container combinations that reflect the reader's personal style.

6. Edible Small Space Gardens

Explore the world of edible small space gardening. Discuss the possibilities of growing herbs, vegetables, and even fruit trees in containers or compact garden beds. Share tips on companion planting to maximize yields.

7. Microgreens and Herbs

Highlight the suitability of small spaces for growing microgreens and herbs. Explain how these fast-growing and flavorful plants can be cultivated indoors or on windowsills, providing fresh ingredients year-round.

8. Vertical Herb Gardens

Provide instructions on creating vertical herb gardens using wall-mounted planters or repurposed pallets. Share herb combinations that are both culinary delights and aromatic garden features.

9. Succulent and Cacti Gardens

Discuss the charm of succulents and cacti in small spaces. Offer tips on potting these low-maintenance plants and creating striking arrangements that require minimal care.

10. Indoor Gardening Secrets

Delve into the world of indoor gardening. Explain how small spaces can be transformed into thriving indoor gardens with proper lighting, humidity control, and plant selection. Discuss the benefits of indoor air purification through plants.

11. Hanging Gardens

Explore hanging gardens as a creative solution for small spaces. Provide step-by-step instructions for crafting hanging planters and ideas for suspending them from ceilings, hooks, or beams.

12. Vertical Vegetable Gardens

Guide readers on vertical vegetable gardening. Share techniques for growing vegetables like tomatoes, cucumbers, and peppers on trellises or garden walls. Discuss the advantages of vertical gardening, including better air circulation and pest management.

13. Windowsill Gardens

Encourage readers to make the most of windowsill space. Offer tips on selecting suitable windowsill planters and growing herbs, small vegetables, or ornamental plants that thrive in indoor sunlight.

14. Lighting and Irrigation

Discuss the importance of adequate lighting and irrigation in small space gardening. Explain the different types of grow lights available for indoor gardens and the best practices for watering container plants.

15. Small Space Garden Design

Address garden design principles for small spaces. Encourage readers to plan their gardens with care, considering factors like color schemes, plant heights, and the use of focal points to create visually appealing small gardens.

16. Vertical Garden Structures

Explore vertical garden structures like living walls and modular systems. Discuss how these innovative solutions can turn walls into vibrant green canvases and offer additional insulation for outdoor spaces.

17. Maintenance and Pruning

Provide guidance on garden maintenance and pruning in small spaces. Explain the importance of regular care, including deadheading flowers, removing diseased leaves, and trimming back overgrown plants.

18. Pest and Disease Management

Discuss strategies for pest and disease management in small space gardens. Encourage organic and environmentally friendly methods to protect plants without harming the environment.

19. Year-Round Gardening

Share tips on extending the gardening season in small spaces. Discuss techniques such as using cloches, row covers, and indoor gardening to enjoy fresh produce and blooms throughout the year.

20. Celebrate the Beauty of Small Gardens

End your chapter by celebrating the beauty and charm of small gardens. Remind readers that small spaces can be transformed into havens of tranquility, creativity, and natural beauty, and that the joy of gardening knows no bounds.

By incorporating these additional tips and tricks, writers can create a comprehensive guide to gardening for small spaces that empowers readers to turn even the tiniest corners of their homes into vibrant and thriving gardens. Small space gardening is a testament to the ingenuity and resilience of nature, and with the right knowledge, readers can cultivate their own green oases regardless of the limitations of space.

Chapter 16: Learning a Rare Language

Guide language enthusiasts on the journey of learning a rare language. Share language resources, tips for efficient learning, and cultural insights related to these languages.

1. Embrace the Challenge

Begin your chapter by emphasizing the excitement and challenge of learning a rare language. Encourage readers to view it as a rewarding journey that provides access to rich cultural experiences.

2. Language Selection

Discuss the importance of carefully choosing a rare language to learn. Suggest resources or websites where readers can explore a variety of rare languages and select the one that resonates with them the most.

3. Finding Language Resources

Guide readers on where to find language resources for rare languages. Recommend online language learning platforms, textbooks, dictionaries, and courses that offer rare language options.

4. Native Speakers and Tutors

Encourage readers to seek out native speakers or tutors of the rare language they are learning. Emphasize the value of practicing with someone who can provide authentic pronunciation and cultural insights.

5. Language Learning Apps

Discuss the availability of language learning apps for rare languages. Share information about apps that offer interactive lessons, pronunciation practice, and language exercises specific to these languages.

6. Cultural Immersion

Highlight the importance of cultural immersion alongside language learning. Encourage readers to explore music, films, literature, and cuisine related to the rare language's culture to deepen their understanding and appreciation.

7. Language Communities

Introduce readers to online language communities and forums dedicated to rare languages. These platforms can connect learners with native speakers, provide learning resources, and offer valuable support and advice.

8. Consistency and Practice

Emphasize the importance of consistency and daily practice in language learning. Encourage readers to set achievable goals and create a structured study routine to maintain progress.

9. Learning Materials

Provide recommendations for rare language learning materials such as textbooks, workbooks, and online courses. Explain the significance of selecting materials that suit their learning style and level.

10. Pronunciation Mastery

Discuss the challenge of mastering pronunciation in rare languages. Suggest techniques such as listening to native speakers, practicing tongue-twisters, and using pronunciation guides.

11. Language Exchange Partners

Encourage readers to find language exchange partners who are interested in learning their native language in exchange for teaching the rare language. Language exchanges offer valuable speaking practice and cultural exchange.

12. Language Challenges

Explain that learning a rare language may come with unique challenges, such as limited learning resources and fewer opportunities for practice. Offer strategies for overcoming these obstacles and staying motivated.

13. Cultural Sensitivity

Emphasize the importance of cultural sensitivity when learning a rare language. Encourage readers to learn about cultural norms, etiquette, and traditions to foster respectful interactions.

14. Documenting Progress

Suggest methods for documenting language learning progress. Encourage readers to keep language journals, record audio clips of their speech, and track vocabulary and grammar milestones.

15. Setting Realistic Goals

Guide readers in setting realistic language learning goals. Encourage them to establish short-term and long-term objectives that align with their language proficiency aspirations.

16. Language Travel

Discuss the benefits of language travel to regions where the rare language is spoken. Share tips on planning language immersion trips, including accommodation, local contacts, and cultural experiences.

17. Language Certification

Explain the value of obtaining language certifications for rare languages. Discuss recognized language proficiency exams and how they can enhance career opportunities or academic pursuits.

18. Celebrate Progress

Encourage readers to celebrate their language learning milestones. Highlight the importance of acknowledging their achievements, no matter how small, to stay motivated and positive.

19. Preserving Rare Languages

Discuss the role of language learners in preserving rare languages. Encourage readers to support language revitalization efforts and engage with local communities to contribute positively.

20. Share Personal Experiences

End your chapter by sharing personal experiences or success stories of individuals who have successfully learned rare languages. These anecdotes can inspire and motivate readers on their language learning journey.

By incorporating these additional tips and tricks, writers can create a comprehensive guide on learning a rare language that not only equips readers with language skills but also fosters cultural appreciation and cross-cultural connections. Learning a rare language is a remarkable and enriching endeavor that can lead to a deeper understanding of the world's linguistic and cultural diversity.

Chapter 17: Antique Collecting and Appraisal

Educate readers on the world of antique collecting. Discuss identifying valuable antiques, assessing their condition, and navigating the antique market.

1. The Passion for Antiques

Begin your chapter by highlighting the passion and intrigue that surrounds antique collecting. Encourage readers to explore their interests and embark on a journey through time and history.

2. Understanding Antiques

Educate readers about what qualifies as an antique. Explain that antiques are typically defined as objects that are at least 100 years old. However, note that the classification may vary depending on the field of collecting.

3. Diverse Collecting Categories

Introduce readers to the diverse categories of antique collecting. Discuss popular categories like furniture, ceramics, glassware, jewelry, coins, textiles, and fine art. Encourage readers to explore a niche that resonates with their interests.

4. Identifying Valuable Antiques

Offer guidance on identifying valuable antiques. Explain factors such as rarity, historical significance, craftsmanship, and provenance that contribute to an antique's value. Share tips on conducting research to determine an item's historical context.

5. Assessing Condition

Discuss the importance of assessing the condition of antiques. Emphasize that the condition greatly affects an antique's value. Provide insights into recognizing signs of wear, restoration, or damage.

6. Antique Appraisal Basics

Introduce readers to the basics of antique appraisal. Explain the role of professional appraisers and how they assess the value of antiques. Suggest reliable sources for finding certified appraisers.

7. DIY Appraisal Techniques

Share DIY appraisal techniques that readers can use to estimate the value of their antiques. Discuss methods like online research, price guides, and comparing similar items in auctions or antique shops.

8. Preservation and Care

Guide readers on the preservation and care of antiques. Explain how to protect antiques from environmental factors like humidity, sunlight, and pests. Share tips for cleaning and maintaining antique items.

9. Authenticity Verification

Discuss the importance of verifying the authenticity of antiques. Explain common methods used to authenticate items, such as examining marks, signatures, and conducting scientific testing when necessary.

10. Antique Market Trends

Educate readers about current antique market trends. Discuss how market demand for specific categories and styles of antiques can fluctuate over time. Encourage readers to stay informed about market dynamics.

11. Buying Antiques

Offer tips for buying antiques wisely. Discuss strategies for finding reputable antique dealers, attending auctions, and negotiating prices. Emphasize the importance of doing due diligence before making a purchase.

12. Selling Antiques

Guide readers on selling antiques effectively. Explain the options available, such as consignment, auctions, or online platforms. Share tips for accurately pricing and marketing antique items for sale.

13. Restoring and Refinishing

Discuss the ethical considerations of restoring and refinishing antiques. Encourage readers to preserve the original character of antique pieces whenever possible and to seek professional restoration when needed.

14. Appraisal for Insurance

Explain the importance of getting antiques appraised for insurance purposes. Encourage readers to periodically update their appraisals to ensure their valuable antiques are adequately covered.

15. Documenting Collections

Encourage readers to document their antique collections. Explain the benefits of maintaining detailed records, including photographs, descriptions, provenance, and appraisals for each item.

16. Joining Collecting Communities

Suggest that readers join antique collecting communities, whether in person or online. These communities provide opportunities to learn from experienced collectors, share knowledge, and network.

17. Ethical Collecting

Discuss the ethical considerations of antique collecting, such as avoiding the purchase of stolen or looted artifacts. Encourage readers to research the provenance of items and support efforts to repatriate stolen cultural heritage.

18. The Joy of Discovery

Emphasize the joy of discovery in antique collecting. Encourage readers to relish the thrill of finding hidden treasures and uncovering the stories behind each antique.

19. Antiques as Investments

Discuss antiques as potential investments. Explain that while antiques can appreciate in value, they should also be enjoyed for their historical and aesthetic significance.

20. Passing Down the Legacy

End your chapter by encouraging readers to consider the legacy of their antique collections. Suggest ways to pass down knowledge and cherished pieces to the next generation, ensuring that the love for antiques endures.

By incorporating these additional tips and tricks, writers can create a comprehensive guide to antique collecting and appraisal that not only equips readers with valuable knowledge but also fosters a deep appreciation for history, craftsmanship, and the art of preserving the past. Antique collecting is a rewarding journey through time, and with the right guidance, readers can embark on this adventure with confidence and passion.

Chapter 18: Entrepreneurial Biographies

Explore the lives of successful entrepreneurs. Share their inspiring stories, business insights, and the lessons readers can apply to their own entrepreneurial ventures.

1. The Power of Role Models

Begin your chapter by emphasizing the power of role models in entrepreneurship. Explain how reading about successful entrepreneurs can inspire and motivate readers to pursue their own business ventures.

2. Diverse Entrepreneurial Stories

Introduce readers to the diversity of entrepreneurial stories. Discuss entrepreneurs from various backgrounds, industries, and time periods. Highlight that success can be achieved through different paths.

3. Selection Criteria

Explain your criteria for selecting the entrepreneurs to feature in the chapter. Consider factors such as their impact on their respective industries, innovation, philanthropy, and the lessons their stories offer to aspiring entrepreneurs.

4. In-Depth Biographical Insights

Provide readers with in-depth biographical insights into each entrepreneur's life. Discuss their early years, education, career beginnings, and the pivotal moments that led them to entrepreneurship.

5. Entrepreneurial Challenges

Delve into the challenges and obstacles that each entrepreneur faced on their journey to success. Explore topics like financial setbacks, competition, failures, and how they persevered.

6. Key Business Ventures

Highlight the key business ventures and projects that defined each entrepreneur's career. Explain the industry, products, or services they pioneered or excelled in.

7. Innovation and Vision

Discuss the innovation and vision that set each entrepreneur apart. Emphasize their ability to identify market gaps, develop groundbreaking ideas, and adapt to changing landscapes.

8. Leadership and Team Building

Explore the leadership qualities of the featured entrepreneurs. Discuss their approaches to team building, management styles, and the values they instilled in their organizations.

9. Customer-Centric Approaches

Examine the customer-centric approaches employed by successful entrepreneurs. Discuss how they prioritized customer needs, feedback, and satisfaction to build lasting businesses.

10. Risk-Taking and Resilience

Highlight the risk-taking mindset and resilience of entrepreneurs. Share stories of bold decisions, calculated risks, and how they bounced back from setbacks.

11. Lessons Learned

Summarize the key lessons readers can learn from each entrepreneur's story. Discuss themes like innovation, determination, adaptability, and the importance of continuous learning.

12. Ethical Business Practices

Discuss the ethical business practices of the featured entrepreneurs. Highlight their commitment to integrity, transparency, and social responsibility.

13. Impact Beyond Business

Explore the entrepreneurs' impact beyond the business world. Discuss their philanthropic efforts, contributions to society, and the legacies they've built.

14. Overcoming Failures

Share stories of how entrepreneurs overcame failures and setbacks. Explain the resilience and determination that allowed them to turn challenges into opportunities.

15. Personal Growth and Development

Discuss the personal growth and development of the entrepreneurs. Explore how their journeys influenced their character, values, and perspectives.

16. Adaptation to Change

Emphasize the ability of successful entrepreneurs to adapt to change and evolving markets. Discuss how they navigated disruptions and remained relevant.

17. Succession and Legacy Planning

Share insights into succession planning and the long-term legacies of the featured entrepreneurs. Explain how they ensured the continuity of their businesses.

18. Practical Application

Encourage readers to reflect on the lessons from each entrepreneurial biography and consider how they can apply these insights to their own business ventures or career paths.

19. Resources for Further Learning

Provide readers with resources for further learning, such as books, documentaries, interviews, and websites related to each entrepreneur. These resources can allow readers to delve deeper into the lives and achievements of these business leaders.

20. Encourage Entrepreneurial Action

End your chapter by encouraging readers to act on their entrepreneurial aspirations. Emphasize that while learning from successful entrepreneurs is valuable, taking the first steps toward their own ventures is essential to their entrepreneurial journey.

By incorporating these additional tips and tricks, writers can create a comprehensive guide to entrepreneurial biographies that not only inspires readers but also equips them with valuable insights and lessons from the lives of remarkable business leaders. Entrepreneurial biographies offer a wealth of wisdom and inspiration for those seeking to make their mark in the world of business and innovation.

Chapter 19: Mental Health and Wellness for Men

Address the unique mental health challenges men face. Provide strategies for stress management, emotional well-being, and seeking support when needed.

1. Understanding the Stigma

Acknowledge the stigma surrounding men's mental health. Start by discussing the societal pressures and expectations that often discourage men from seeking help. Emphasize the importance of breaking this stigma and normalizing conversations about mental well-being.

2. The Unique Challenges Men Face

Highlight the unique mental health challenges that men may encounter. Discuss issues such as toxic masculinity, emotional suppression, and the reluctance to seek help due to perceived weakness. Explain how these challenges can impact men's mental well-being.

3. Promoting Emotional Expression

Encourage men to embrace emotional expression. Stress that it's okay to feel a wide range of emotions, and that vulnerability is a strength, not a weakness. Share stories of men who have benefited from opening up about their feelings.

4. The Power of Connection

Discuss the importance of building strong social connections. Explain how nurturing meaningful relationships can provide emotional support and reduce feelings of isolation. Offer tips for maintaining and fostering friendships and family bonds.

5. Stress Management Strategies

Provide practical stress management strategies tailored to men's needs. Explore techniques like mindfulness, deep breathing exercises, and physical activities such as sports or yoga. Highlight the role of stress reduction in maintaining mental wellness.

6. Physical Health and Mental Well-Being

Explain the connection between physical health and mental well-being. Discuss the importance of regular exercise, a balanced diet, and quality sleep in promoting positive mental health for men. Offer tips for maintaining a healthy lifestyle.

7. Seeking Professional Help

Address the misconception that seeking professional help is a sign of weakness. Stress the importance of reaching out to mental health professionals when needed. Provide information on different types of therapy and how to find the right therapist.

8. Coping with Trauma

Acknowledge that men may experience trauma that affects their mental health. Discuss coping mechanisms and the importance of seeking therapy or support groups for trauma survivors. Share stories of resilience and recovery.

9. Encouraging Self-Care

Promote self-care practices as essential for men's mental wellness. Explain the benefits of taking time for oneself, pursuing hobbies, and engaging in relaxation techniques. Offer self-care ideas that resonate with men, such as woodworking, journaling, or fishing.

10. Role of Work-Life Balance

Discuss the role of work-life balance in mental health. Emphasize the importance of setting boundaries at work, taking breaks, and prioritizing personal time. Share strategies for managing job-related stress.

11. Substance Abuse Awareness

Address the issue of substance abuse and its impact on men's mental health. Provide information on the signs of addiction and resources for seeking help. Encourage men to seek support for substance abuse issues.

12. Mental Health Check-Ins

Promote regular mental health check-ins. Encourage men to assess their emotional well-being and seek help if they notice persistent changes in mood or behavior. Share self-assessment tools and resources.

13. Redefining Masculinity

Discuss the importance of redefining masculinity in a way that embraces emotional intelligence, empathy, and self-compassion. Challenge traditional stereotypes that limit men's emotional expression and well-being.

14. Balancing Responsibilities

Offer advice on balancing responsibilities such as work, family, and personal life. Discuss time management techniques and the importance of setting realistic goals to reduce stress and maintain mental wellness.

15. Cultivating Resilience

Explore the concept of resilience and how it can be cultivated. Share stories of men who have overcome adversity and developed resilience. Provide strategies for building resilience, including problem-solving skills and positive thinking.

16. Cultural Sensitivity

Acknowledge the cultural factors that may influence men's mental health. Discuss the intersection of culture, identity, and mental wellness, and emphasize the importance of culturally sensitive approaches to support.

17. Holistic Well-Being

Encourage a holistic approach to well-being that encompasses physical, emotional, and social aspects of life. Stress that mental health is an integral part of overall health, and that seeking balance in all areas is essential.

18. Supportive Resources

Provide a comprehensive list of resources where men can find support, including hotlines, counseling services, online communities, and mental health organizations. Ensure that the resources are easily accessible.

19. Stories of Triumph

Share inspiring stories of men who have overcome mental health challenges and thrived. These stories can serve as powerful examples of hope and resilience, showing readers that recovery is possible.

20. Encouraging Conversations

End the chapter by emphasizing the importance of ongoing conversations about men's mental health. Encourage readers to share their own experiences, seek support, and support others in their journey towards well-being.

Incorporating these additional tips and tricks into your writing on the topic of mental health and wellness for men will allow you to provide comprehensive guidance and support. Remember that addressing men's mental health is a crucial step in promoting overall well-being and breaking down the barriers that prevent men from seeking help when needed. By creating a safe and understanding space, your writing can make a meaningful impact on the mental health of men everywhere.

Chapter 20: Unconventional Hobbies

Celebrate niche hobbies like beekeeping and blacksmithing. Offer beginner's guides, safety tips, and insights into the satisfaction these hobbies can bring.

1. Embracing Unconventional Hobbies

Begin your chapter by highlighting the charm of unconventional hobbies. Emphasize that these unique pursuits often provide a break from the ordinary and allow individuals to explore their passions.

2. A World of Niche Hobbies

Introduce readers to the diverse world of niche hobbies. Discuss a range of unconventional interests, from beekeeping and blacksmithing to other intriguing pursuits like urban foraging, letterpress printing, or falconry.

3. Finding the Right Hobby

Offer guidance on how to discover the right unconventional hobby for individual interests and preferences. Encourage readers to explore their curiosities and consider what resonates with them.

4. Getting Started

Provide beginner's guides for each hobby. Explain the basic equipment or tools needed, safety precautions, and initial steps to take when starting out in the chosen hobby.

5. Safety First

Discuss safety as a paramount concern in unconventional hobbies. Emphasize the importance of proper training, protective gear, and adherence to safety guidelines to prevent accidents or injuries.

6. Beekeeping Basics

Dive into the world of beekeeping. Share insights on setting up beehives, selecting the right bee species, and maintaining a healthy bee colony. Highlight the role of bees in pollination and honey production.

7. Blacksmithing for Beginners

Guide readers on their journey into blacksmithing. Explain the essential tools, materials, and techniques involved in shaping metal. Share safety tips and recommended resources for learning blacksmithing skills.

8. Urban Foraging Adventures

Explore the fascinating hobby of urban foraging. Explain how to identify edible wild plants, mushrooms, and fruits in urban environments. Emphasize the importance of ethical foraging practices.

9. Letterpress Printing Artistry

Introduce readers to the art of letterpress printing. Discuss the history of letterpress, the necessary equipment, and the joy of creating handmade, tactile printed materials.

10. The World of Falconry

Delve into the world of falconry. Share the unique bond between falconers and their birds of prey. Explain the process of training, caring for, and flying raptors for hunting or sport.

11. Satisfactions of Unconventional Hobbies

Discuss the satisfactions and rewards that come with unconventional hobbies. Explore the sense of connection with nature, the tactile satisfaction of working with one's hands, and the meditative aspects of these pursuits.

12. Overcoming Challenges

Acknowledge the challenges that enthusiasts may encounter in unconventional hobbies. Share stories of how hobbyists have overcome obstacles and developed their skills over time.

13. Community and Camaraderie

Highlight the sense of community and camaraderie that often accompanies unconventional hobbies. Discuss how enthusiasts come together through clubs, forums, and events to share knowledge and experiences.

14. Benefits Beyond the Hobby

Explore the benefits that extend beyond the hobby itself. Discuss how these pursuits can lead to increased mindfulness, reduced stress, and a sense of accomplishment.

15. Preservation of Traditions

Emphasize how unconventional hobbies often preserve traditional crafts and skills that might otherwise be lost. Discuss the importance of passing down knowledge to future generations.

16. Sustainability and Self-Reliance

Discuss the sustainability and self-reliance aspects of some unconventional hobbies. Explain how activities like beekeeping, urban foraging, and blacksmithing can promote self-sufficiency and sustainability.

17. Unconventional Hobbies as Creative Outlets

Explore how unconventional hobbies serve as creative outlets for enthusiasts. Discuss the artistic and expressive aspects of pursuits like letterpress printing and falconry.

18. Encouraging Exploration

Encourage readers to explore unconventional hobbies as a means of discovering new passions and interests. Remind them that these hobbies offer opportunities for personal growth and learning.

19. Resources for Enthusiasts

Provide readers with resources for further exploration. Suggest books, websites, local clubs or groups, and workshops where they can delve deeper into their chosen unconventional hobby.

20. Celebrating Uniqueness

End your chapter by celebrating the uniqueness of unconventional hobbies. Emphasize that these pursuits reflect the rich diversity of human interests and the joy that comes from exploring the road less traveled.

By incorporating these additional tips and tricks, writers can create a comprehensive guide on unconventional hobbies that not only introduces readers to fascinating pursuits but also inspires them to embrace their own passions and explore the world of niche hobbies. Unconventional hobbies offer a gateway to creativity, fulfillment, and a deeper connection with the world around us.

Conclusion

Throughout this guide, you've explored a wide range of topics, from sustainable living guides to entrepreneurial biographies and everything in between. As you conclude your exploration of these niches and continue your writing journey, there are some key takeaways to keep in mind.

1. Writing Is an Adventure

Your journey into these 20 niches is an adventure filled with discovery, learning, and creativity. Writing allows you to explore different worlds, share knowledge, and connect with readers who share your interests. Embrace the thrill of this journey.

2. Passion Is Your North Star

Passion is the driving force behind compelling writing. Whether you're delving into sustainable living, entrepreneurial biographies, or beekeeping, your enthusiasm for the topic will shine through in your words. Write about what genuinely excites you, and your readers will feel that enthusiasm.

3. Authenticity Matters

In every niche, authenticity is key. Readers appreciate writers who speak from the heart and share their genuine experiences and insights. Be true to your voice and beliefs, and your writing will resonate with those who share your perspective.

4. Know Your Audience

Understanding your audience is crucial. Take the time to research and connect with the people who are interested in the niche you're writing about. Consider their needs, questions, and preferences, and tailor your content to address them effectively.

5. Dive Deep into Research

Each niche you explore will require in-depth research. Whether you're writing about beekeeping techniques, the life of an entrepreneur, or the art of blacksmithing, strive for accuracy and thoroughness in your content. Readers value well-researched, informative writing.

6. Be a Storyteller

Storytelling is a powerful tool in writing. Even in non-fiction niches like personal finance or letterpress printing, stories humanize your content and make it relatable. Share anecdotes, case studies, and real-life experiences to engage your readers on a personal level.

7. Value Simplicity and Clarity

In niches that may involve technical or specialized knowledge, remember the importance of simplicity and clarity in your writing. Make complex concepts accessible to your readers through clear explanations and relatable examples.

8. Keep Evolving

Writing is a journey of growth and evolution. As you explore these niches, you'll continually refine your craft. Don't be afraid to embrace change, experiment with new styles, and learn from both successes and setbacks.

9. Embrace the Niche's Unique Charms

Each niche you write about has its own unique charm and community. Whether it's the tight-knit world of beekeepers or the dynamic realm of entrepreneurial innovation, immerse yourself in the culture and values of the niche to better connect with your readers.

10. Build Your Expertise

While your passion is your starting point, strive to build expertise in the niches you explore. Becoming an authority in a particular field not only enhances your writing but also fosters trust with your readers.

11. Networking Matters

Connect with fellow enthusiasts and experts in the niches you write about. Networking can lead to valuable insights, collaboration opportunities, and a deeper understanding of the niche.

12. Seek Feedback and Improve

Welcome feedback from your readers, peers, or mentors. Constructive criticism can help you refine your writing skills and cater to your audience's needs more effectively.

13. Persistence Is Key

Like any journey, your writing journey may have its challenges and obstacles. Persistence is key to overcoming these hurdles. Stay committed to your craft and your passion for writing.

14. Impact and Inspiration

Remember that your writing has the power to inspire and make a positive impact. Whether you're helping someone start a new hobby, learn about an unconventional interest, or gain insights into sustainable living, your words can shape perspectives and change lives.

15. Happy Writing!

Lastly, remember that writing is not just a craft but a joy. As you explore these niches and continue your writing journey, savor the process. The act of writing itself can be immensely satisfying and fulfilling.

In conclusion, congratulations on your journey through these diverse niches. Writing is a lifelong adventure, and with each niche you explore, you deepen your understanding of the world and your ability to connect with others. Stay true to your voice, continue learning, and keep your readers' needs and interests at the forefront of your writing journey. Happy writing, and may your words continue to inspire and enlighten those who read them.